CW01563542

THE 7 HABITS OF HIGHLY EFFECTIVE PEOPLE

The keys to success

Summary & Analysis of
Stephen R. Covey's book

Written by Soraya Belghazi
Translated by Ciaran Traynor

Book Review

80003796786

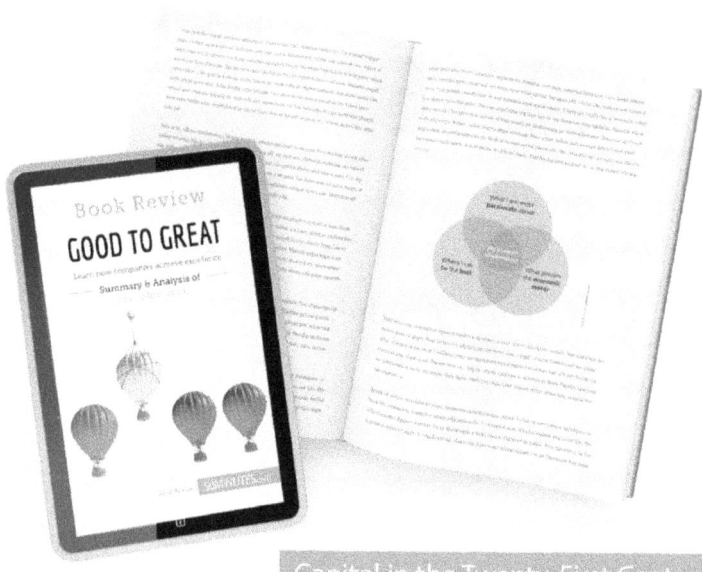

50MINUTES.com

BUSINESS WISDOM
IN THE PALM OF YOUR HAND!

Capital in the Twenty-First Century

First Things First

Rich Dad Poor Dad

The Speed of Trust

www.50minutes.com

THE 7 HABITS OF HIGHLY EFFECTIVE PEOPLE

INCREASE YOUR PERSONAL EFFICIENCY WITHOUT LOSING SIGHT OF WHO YOU ARE

Habits play a very important role in our daily lives and have a huge influence on our efficiency... or, on the contrary, our inefficiency. Which good habits can make a positive difference in our lives and how can we get rid of our 'bad' habits?

Ever since it was first published in 1989, Stephen Covey's (American author, businessman and keynote speaker, 1932-2012) *The 7 Habits of Highly Effective People* has become a worldwide bestseller, translated into more than 40 languages and selling more than 25 million copies. Covey taught leadership and management at some of America's most prestigious universities, but it was above all his work as a consultant for several years that allowed him to develop a theoretical, practical approach to personal effectiveness.

The strength of *The 7 Habits of Highly Effective People* lies in the fact that they can be applied to all walks of life, whether the subject in question is personal or professional. The method is customisable in the sense that each habit is tailored to your own personal values. Unlike self-help books which focus on behaviour, Covey's book offers sustainable improvement, because it requires you to work on yourself.

Are you ready to break free of the daily rut and reconsider how you think and act to make the most of your potential?

of leadership. *The 7 Habits of Highly Effective People* is no exception. He mentions the sabbatical year he spent with his family in Hawaii, during which he wrote *The 7 Habits of Highly Effective People*. He also talks about the problems he and his wife Sandra (1957-2012) had with one of their sons, who was doing badly at school.

Following a number of prizes for his contribution to management theory and the publication of many other works exploring aspects related to *The 7 Habits of Highly Effective People*, Covey went back to teaching management at Utah State University in 2010, before dying after a bike accident 16 July 2012 at the age of 79.

CONTEXT

Management and personal development books enjoyed a surge in popularity in the 1980s and 1990s in the United States. *The 7 Habits of Highly Effective People* was part of this success. In this book, Covey adopts several theories developed in the 1960s and 1970s by Peter Drucker (1909-2005), one of the major theorists of management. Drucker was also one of the first people to consider effectiveness as a habit in his 1967 work *The Effective Executive*.

During his doctoral research, Covey looked at a considerable number of works on success and personal development, taking a particular interest in time management and interpersonal communication. In spite of his many 'classic' influences, Covey's approach has a certain originality to it, which goes a long way towards explaining the immediate success of the book.

Firstly, Covey rejects what he calls "the personality ethic", which dominated personal development programmes at the time and involved presenting success as a consequence of personality, image, attitude and behaviour, or as the result of specific techniques and abilities. Those who adhere to personality ethics therefore advise individuals to adopt a positive mental attitude if they want to follow the 'recipe' to success.

Covey denounces this type of advice as nothing more than a short-term solution, because it does not encourage you to understand yourself but rather to imitate those who you admire. On the contrary, he advocates a return to the classic theories of the 18th and 19th centuries aiming to develop "character ethics". Unlike personality, character refers to an individual's internal values, rather than their external behaviour. It is based on values such as integrity, humility and loyalty, linked to the famous "virtues" lauded by Benjamin Franklin in his autobiography. Indeed, Covey is convinced that individuals tend to trust people when they know their character, as opposed to their behaviour.

The second original aspect of the Covey method is that it encompasses both the private and professional sphere. Unlike management works such as *The One Minute Manager* (1980) by Ken Blanchard and Spencer Johnson, to take but one example, Covey's work is intended for both individuals and organisations. The examples cited in the book are taken from his personal experience as a husband, father, lecturer, coach, manager and business consultant. Thanks to their general, universal application, the seven habits in

With this introduction to *The 7 Habits of Highly Effective People*, learn about the cornerstones of Covey's method and discover how it can help you to take your life back into your own hands in just 50 minutes.

KEY INFORMATION

- **Reference**: Covey, S. (2004) *The 7 Habits of Highly Effective People*. New York: Free Press.
- **1st edition**: 1989
- **Author**: Stephen Richards Covey (management professor, coach and entrepreneur. Born 23 October 1932 in Salt Lake City, United States, and died 16 July 2012 in Idaho Falls in the United States)
- **Key words**:
  - **Emotional Bank Balance**: how much others trust us based on our past actions, and in particular on our ability to interact with them in a selfless, empathetic manner.
  - **Integrity**: the ability to act every day in accordance with your values.
  - **Leadership**: the ability to act proactively to positively influence others, while always keeping your objective in mind.
  - **Synergy**: the bringing together of ideas, resources or actions to achieve a result greater than the sum of its parts.

CONTEXT

Stephen Covey was born in 1932 in Utah, right in the heart-land of America, and grew up in a practising Mormon family. An MBA (Master of Business Administration) graduate of Harvard University, he wrote his doctoral thesis on religious education at Brigham Young University. He also taught at Brigham Young before launching his own consultancy business in 1985.

Thanks to the worldwide success of *The 7 Habits of Highly Effective People*, published in 1989, he developed his coaching, training and consultancy work for different businesses, organisations and individuals.

In 1997, he merged his business with Hyrum W. Smith's company Franklin Quest. Like Covey, Smith is a Mormon and an expert in personal efficiency, known as the creator of the Franklin Planner, a time management tool inspired by Benjamin Franklin (1706-1790), one of the Founding Fathers of the United States. In his autobiography, he made a list of the "13 virtues" which have inspired many American ethical and personal development theorists, including Smith and Covey. Their business, named FranklinCovey, is listed on the New York Stock Exchange and offers coaching and strategic advice services throughout the world.

The father of nine children, Covey regularly brings up his family life in his works to illustrate different principles

the book can be used by the general public in a wide variety of situations.

SUMMARY OF *THE 7 HABITS OF HIGHLY EFFECTIVE PEOPLE*

THE FOUR KEY PRINCIPLES AT THE HEART OF THE SEVEN HABITS

To understand the range of Covey's seven habits, it is a good idea to define a few notions in advance. The author bases his whole approach on several fundamental principles which still tend to be overlooked.

The difference between character and personality

The notion of 'character' is at the heart of Covey's book, as he views it, and not personality, as the reason for success. Instead of focusing on 'external' displays of behaviour, it refers instead to the individual's fundamental values such as integrity, loyalty, temperance, courage, justice, patience and simplicity. Although these character traits were considered to be extremely important throughout the 18th and 19th centuries, they tended to be neglected by theorists from the early 20th century.

Adopting new habits must therefore come from an 'inner'" desire. You cannot simply imitate successful people and hope for the same results. On the contrary, you have to act in accordance with your own values and work on understanding yourself. As Covey highlights, it is people's characters which allow us to truly trust them. What we are tells others far more about us than what we say or do.

A Paradigm Shift

A paradigm is a framework or model of thinking. In a way, it is the way we perceive, understand and interpret the world.

Covey talks about "mental maps" to underline the fact that the same situation is never seen in the same way by two different people. We create these "maps" in order to better understand our environment, but in the end they are nothing more than imperfect reflections of reality. Which is why there are as many maps as there are mapmakers...

In the 1960s, the American philosopher Thomas Kuhn (1922-1996) showed how almost all great scientific discoveries were the result of breaking away from tradition and old ways of thinking. Consequently, Covey talks about "Paradigm Shifts", such as when the Polish astronomer Nicolaus Copernicus (1473-1543) claimed that the Sun is at the centre of the universe and not the Earth, completely shattering our perception of the world and humans' place within it.

Most individuals go through Paradigm Shifts at key periods in their lives. A birth or a death, for example, can lead us to review our priorities and break away from our old way of thinking or functioning. The notion of the paradigm is therefore crucial to help us to understand what habits we are enslaved by.

Covey himself sums this up very well: "The way we see the problem is the problem" (p. 21). Changing your attitude will only have a limited impact on your daily routine, while reviewing your basic paradigms will allow you to make

life-altering changes.

Your Circle of Influence

Covey believes in "natural laws": unchangeable principles which determine the effectiveness of human action. These principles are neither values, nor practices, because these things can change. Natural laws are basic parameters, undeniable evidence which defines human actions, such as the principle of justice and human dignity. At the same time, Covey suggests that people have free will and can therefore make decisions about their lives based on the way that they respond to given situations.

The difficulty therefore consists in determining the nature and the extent of each individual's "Circle of Influence". In other words, we have to acknowledge that each of us only has true influence over a limited number of things and people, which make up our Circle of Influence. However, our Circle of Concern is normally larger than our Circle of Influence. Some of the subjects that are important to us and make up our Circle of Concern are beyond our control, such as the health of a loved one at the end of their life.

In order to be more effective, we have to focus our efforts on our Circle of Influence and avoid spending time on projects that are doomed to failure from the start. Each of these seven habits aims to identify our individual Circle of Influence and extend it as much as we possibly can.

Your Emotional Bank Account

The common denominator of the fourth, fifth and sixth habits is the notion of your "Emotional Bank Account". This metaphor was developed by Covey to help us to "measure" the degree of trust we give people.

The idea is that our interactions with other people either increase, or on the contrary decrease, our Emotional Bank Balance with these people. Acts of kindness and selfless offers of help allow us to increase the balance in our bank account. This means that whoever is benefiting from our deposits is likely to do the same for us if need be, or even to forgive our mistakes, in light of our past exchanges.

On the other hand, when we regularly ask someone for help without ever giving anything in return, our Emotional Bank Balance decreases accordingly, and it is likely that they will be less disposed to help us when we need it most. Trying to increase your Emotional Bank Balance in each human relationship is important, whether in your family or professional life, and for Covey is the basis of success and interdependence.

THE SEVEN HABITS

After defining the basic notions, it is now time to present the famous "seven habits" which are at the heart of Covey's method. Here is a general summary:

Private Victories
1. Be Proactive 2. Begin with the End in Mind 3. Put First Things First
Public Victories
4. Think Win-Win 5. Seek First to Understand, Then to Be Understood 6. Synergise
Renewal
7. Sharpen the Saw

Habit 1 – Be Proactive

This first habit primarily involves developing a personal mission and searching for ways to put it into practice on a daily basis. Covey is not a fan of determinism, or the idea that we are conditioned to respond in a certain manner in a given situation. On the contrary, he considers that freedom comes precisely from our ability to choose how to react in a given situation. Being proactive does not just mean taking initiative: it means being responsible for your own life and your own choices. For Covey, "our behavior is a function of our decisions, not our conditions" (p. 39).

Habit 2 – Begin with the End in Mind

Habit 2 involves developing a strategic vision, and more generally being a leader. In order to connect with our fundamental values and make good choices, Covey challenges us

to think about our death, what we want people to think of us, and the meaning that we want to give our lives.

Thinking about the result from the very beginning is a good way to ensure that our daily actions do not go against our values and the criteria that we have defined as important for success. Whether at an individual or a personal level, everyone has their own definition of success and has to use it to guide their actions.

However, Covey goes one step further with the principle that "all things are created twice" (p. 54):

- first comes mental creation, meaning the idea;
- then comes the second, physical creation, which is the concrete realisation of this idea.

In order to be effective, a leader must anticipate the realisation of their idea. The second habit, which is related to ideas and leadership, is therefore closely connected to Habit 3, which is linked to realisation and management. In business, employees are often shut up in a paradigm of management and daily management. They do not take an overall look at their decisions and strategic reflection is neglected. However, being truly effective is impossible without becoming a better leader. What is the point in improving processes or methods if we have the wrong objective?

Habit 3 – Put First Things First

This habit may seem obvious at first but, in reality, doing things in the right order requires a certain amount of dis-

cipline. People naturally favour easy, pleasant tasks to the detriment of tasks which require more effort, even if these tasks would bring them closer to their objectives. For Covey, being able to manage yourself demands integrity, meaning the courage to act according to your values. After visualising your objectives (the 'final' phase of Habit 2), you have to be able to define your priorities and work on carrying them out.

Ordered principles

The order of the seven habits was not chosen at random. Each habit follows on from the previous one. Indeed, in order to be interdependent, you first need to become independent.

- Habits 1, 2 and 3 aim to achieve this independence. Covey talks about "Private Victories" to underline the fact that these first three habits are all about self-management.
- Habits 4, 5 and 6 lead to the next level: "Public Victories". These victories focus on interdependence between several independent individuals. These habits aim to increase your efficiency thanks to rich, productive and long-lasting relationships.

Habit 4 – Think Win-Win

With this fourth habit, Covey invites us to consider each human interaction as a source of mutual benefit, as he believes it is almost always possible to completely satisfy everyone. In other words, Covey rejects the idea that hap-

piness for some people causes unhappiness for others. The secret is our ability to see problems as opportunities to find solutions.

As a result, when a customer complains about a faulty product, a good salesman will not think of the necessary compensation as an unpleasant chore, but as an opportunity to restore their customer's confidence by finding the best solution possible.

Unfortunately, our environment is still strongly influence by this win-lose philosophy. At school, students are judged based on their notes; there are no 'good students' without 'bad students'. In business, employees are often promoted or given pay rises if they perform better than their colleagues. Covey suggests that we question this state of affairs and cooperate instead of competing.

Habit 5 – Seek First to Understand, Then to Be Understood

Empathic communication is the key to Covey's fifth habit. The need to be understood is one of the most universal human feelings. The majority of people think that, in order to have influence, you have to be able to communicate by conveying clear, convincing messages. For Covey, the real influence comes from being able to listen to others.

Too often, we only half listen to others because we are too busy preparing a retort, instead of first trying to understand their point of view. However, when you do this, it is impossible to understand the other person's paradigm or

put yourself in their shoes. By getting ready to fire back an answer, we filter the subject based on our own values and our own experiences, which prevents us from truly empathising with the other person. The challenge is to avoid prematurely judging or interpreting what others are saying. Instead, you should listen in order to understand. This type of listening significantly increases your Emotional Bank Balance and, therefore, your influence.

Habit 6 – Synergise

This sixth habit is, in a way, the result of the first five. It is all about collective intelligence. We can summarise the principle of synergy with the formula 1+1=3. Within a group, the opposition of different ideas often leads to solutions which nobody could ever have reached alone. In practice, searching for synergy leads us to value different opinions, rather than fearing them.

The fact that some companies are trying to diversify their board of directors is the direct consequence of synergy. Opposing points of view allow businesses to find innovative, efficient solutions to their problems. Homogeneity, on the other hand, often deprives organisations of different talents and prevents them from seizing opportunities... which their competitors will not be foolish enough to pass up.

Habit 7 – Sharpen the Saw

The final habit is meant to consolidate all the others. To illustrate this principle of "self-renewal", Covey gives the example of a man trying to cut a tree down with a blunt saw:

would it not be a better idea to sharpen the saw, and then cut down the tree? In response to this question, the man says "I don't have time to sharpen the saw... I'm too busy sawing!" (p. 187). This attitude is typical of individuals who, once they are under pressure, get completely caught up in what they are doing without even questioning the efficiency of their method. However, if you just take a bit of time to reflect on your method and improve it, you will often reach your objective much more efficiently. Therefore, you save time in the long term.

METHODS FOR BETTER SELF-MANAGEMENT

Covey suggests several ways to put the first three habits into practice in order to reach these "Private Victories". There are five recommendations in total.

- **Always respect your own commitments**. An essential part of your Circle of Influence is your ability to keep our own promises. In both your professional life and your private circle, respecting your commitments allows you to increase your integrity and Emotional Bank Balance, but also to stay in control of your life. Moreover, keeping promises you make to yourself is essential if you want to be able to keep your promises to others.
- **Use proactive language, rather than reactive language**. In difficult situations, your own reactions can be more harmful than what has actually happened to you. Changing how you speak is an effective way of reducing the negative impact of certain events on your life. By adopting proactive language, rather than reactive lan-

guage, we encourage our brain to find solutions instead of letting ourselves by overwhelmed by difficulties.

For example, if you have to sacrifice going to a family gathering to finish a task at the office, you might be tempted to make excuses like "I have to stay late at work, I don't have a choice". However, it would be more honest, and far more motivating, to tell the truth and say "I'd love to come but I've decided to stay longer at the office to finish this bit of work, because it's an important task and I want my colleagues to feel that they can count of me during this stressful time at the office. I'm positive we'll be able to finish this project if we just put a little effort into it, so I'll be able to spend more time with you over the course of the following weeks."

- **Work out your personal mission statement**. An essential part of Habit 2 is creating your own personal mission statement. This mission statement must be written down and state what makes you or your business unique. This can help you measure your effectiveness by asking yourself the question: how is what I am preparing to do going to help me to reach my objective, as I formulated it in my personal mission statement?

  For example, FranklinCovey's mission statement is to "Enable Greatness in People and Organizations Everywhere" (FranklinCovey official website).

- **Use visualisation to change your behaviour**. Visualisation is a technique which can help anyone to incorporate their personal mission in their daily lives. It uses the right hemisphere of the brain. In order to get rid of your bad habits, for example your tendency to get annoyed at a colleague who takes a while to understand ins-

tructions, you have to visualise the situation and imagine a more appropriate response based on the values and principles defined in your personal mission statement. If you write the 'script' in advance, all you have it do is act it out when the situation comes up.

Therefore, when you decide to sit down with your colleague and calmly explain the task step by step, so that they will definitely understand, you will find it easier to control your impatience. Visualisation techniques are often used by athletes to mentally train themselves to reach optimal performance.

- **Define your priorities and devote as much time as possible to carrying them out, including the completion of important, but non-urgent tasks**. In order to do this, Covey uses the famous Eisenhower Matrix, inspired by a quote attributed to former US President Eisenhower (1890-1969), which classifies human activity into four broad categories.

The Eisenhower Matrix

The first and second categories of this matrix correspond to important activities that will help us to reach our objectives. We must spend the greatest amount of time on these activities, including those which are important but not urgent. This is the essence of personal effective. Anticipating problems and reflecting on possible improvements will allow us to grow more effective over the long term.

Spending too much time on activities from the third and fourth categories, on the other hand, will often make us stray from our objectives. When possible, we should try to

delegate these activities to other people, or even give them up, in order to concentrate on what is truly important.

METHODS TO COMMUNICATE BETTER WITH OTHERS

Covey distinguishes six main ways to increase your Emotional Bank Balance with others:

- **Try to understand other people's priorities**. Just because you enjoy talking with your colleague for hours on end does not mean that they do too. If you want to increase your Emotional Bank Balance, the person you are making a deposit with also has to appreciate it.
- **Do not neglect the little things**. Little everyday niceties, like a simple hello with a smile, sometimes make all the difference.
- **Respect your promises**. Keeping your word automatically increases your Emotional Bank Balance. Breaking it, on the other hand, will take a big chunk out of your savings.
- **Formulate your expectations clearly**. Poor or unclear communication of your expectations will always end with misunderstandings and, consequently, lost trust.
- **Act with integrity**. Being honest and consistent in what you say is the foundation of trust. Telling someone the opposite of what you say to someone else is being two-faced and implies that you are not trustworthy.
- **Apologise sincerely when you make a "withdrawal" from your account**. Having the courage to admit that you are wrong is essential to keep others' trust.

Once a person has a high enough Emotional Bank Balance, they can use it influence people and get results. However, you cannot simply make demands on other people: you have to look for win-win solutions. In both professional and personal contexts, we often have to negotiate with others before making a decision. A win-win attitude means looking not only for advantageous conditions for yourself, but also the optimal result for others. To do this, Covey recommends including these five elements in every negotiation:

- agreeing on the objective to achieve, rather than on the means to achieve it;
- guidelines to set general principles and constraints;
- the necessary resources, whether financial, technical, human or organisational;
- evaluation and review methods, which will allow you to check whether or not your criteria have been respected;
- the consequences of respecting or not respecting the evaluation criteria.

The first point is particularly important for Covey. Agreeing on objectives to achieve is not only effective in negotiation – it is the basis of all effective delegation. It means you do not need to describe exactly what the person has to do, leaving them free to choose their own means to achieve their objectives. They are given the satisfaction of being able to choose their preferred method and therefore feel responsible for the results.

In practice, this manner of delegating requires a bit more time at the beginning to clarify expectations and ensure that the person understands the objectives and constraints.

However, over the medium-term, the person becomes more independent, which in turn helps us to be more effective.

IMPACT OF *THE 7 HABITS OF HIGHLY EFFECTIVE PEOPLE*

The global success of *The 7 Habits of Highly Effective People* has not spared Covey from criticism.

- He is criticised in particular for recycling existing concepts and spouting truisms (such as "Put First Things First").
- What is more, some people criticise him for his constant use of examples from his personal life, rather than empirical research carried out by scientists or researchers.
- His "all-in-one" approach, which promises to be applicable to both private and professional life, also causes debate, even though Covey demonstrates in a relatively convincing manner that the two aspects often go hand in hand, and that your character and values influence both your personal and professional efficiency.

In his *Guide du leadership* ("Leadership Guide", 2007), Bernard Radon makes a more general criticism of Covey for not taking external influences into account. For Radon, Covey's seven habits can be reduced to one simple phrase: "You can do it if you want to"[1]. In practice, however, will is rarely enough, and people have to take into account a number of different environmental factors. In professional contexts in particular, a rigid company culture which discourages individual initiative can hold an employee back if

---

1. This quotation has been translated by BrightSummaries.com.

they want to use the seven habits to work based on their own values. Basically, as *The Economist* highlighted in its obituary of Stephen Covey in July 2012, combining the works of several effective individuals is not enough to make an effective business. This is why Covey's individualistic perspective must be complemented by a subtler, more complex approach that takes structural and organisational constraints into account.

The ethical dimension of *The 7 Habits of Highly Effective People* has been both lauded and lambasted. The positive side of Covey's approach is that is puts morality back into management and leadership by highlighting the values of integrity, honesty and authenticity. Instead of trying to superficially change our attitude, without considering the nature of the objectives we want to achieve, Covey invites us to reflect on the moral dimension of our actions. For him, true confidence and self-esteem come from being honest with yourself, in accordance with your own values, rather than merely playing a 'role'. However, he is still guilty of a certain amount of religious proselytism in his search for morality. Although the seven habits are formulated in such a way that they can be applied to any individual, whatever their personal convictions, Covey was a staunch Mormon and considered his faith as the foundation of his approach. In his "Personal Note" at the end of the book, he wrote "I believe that there are parts to human nature that cannot be reached by either legislation or education, but require the power of God to deal with" (p. 207).

Paradoxically, *The 7 Habits of Highly Effective People* has

also been targeted by strict Christian groups, who believe that Covey is mistaken in putting man at the centre of his personal development method and not God.

Cove was inspired by a number of theories to create his seven habits. These sources of inspiration come from a variety of disciplines, from literature to psychology, and even the philosophy of science.

In his section on "Private Victories", Covey refers to the autobiographies of famous people such as the previously mentioned Benjamin Franklin and the former Egyptian president Anwar Sadat (1918-1981). Sadat talked about how his stint in a Cairo prison in the 1940s helped him to develop an unwavering strength of character. Viktor Frankl (1905-1997) is another personality who considerably influenced Covey. Frankl was a survivor of the concentration camps and the creator of logotherapy, a form of psychological treatment centred on the 'meaning' of individuals and their spiritual dimension. Habit 2, which advises beginning with the end in mind, is largely inspired by Frankl's approach.

Covey recycles several existing concepts, which can be seen from the fact that:

- Habit 3, "Put First Things First", is directly influenced by the Eisenhower Matrix, which was developed in the 1950s to set priorities by classifying the urgency and importance of different tasks.
- Habit 4, "Think Win-Win", is inspired by the method of

reasonable negotiation advocated by Roger Fisher and William Ury in their famous work *Getting to Yes*, published in 1981. This method involves identifying common interests in order to reach a rational agreement between all parties based on objective criteria.

- Habit 6, "Synergise", refers to the sociologist Kurt Lewin's (1890-1947) force-field analysis, developed in the 1940s. According to this theory, successful change requires rebalancing your driving forces, the factors which push you towards change, and your hindering forces, the forces of resistance which try to preserve the status quo.

Other specialists in personal effectiveness also took inspiration from Covey's work. The practical tools which he developed are now at the heart of FranklinCovey's consultancy and coaching services, but a range of other consultancy businesses have also been inspired, either directly or indirectly, by his approach. Almost 30 years after they were first published, the seven habits are still regularly quoted in management training courses across the world.

Recently, Project Happiness, an American non-profit association which mainly targets students, developed the "7 Happiness Habits", a group of practices which are supposed to reduce anxiety and help you to rediscover meaning and tranquillity in your everyday life. This is obviously a clear nod to Covey's seven habits.

SELLING OUT

Covey has been criticised for excessively 'recycling' his seven habits for purely commercial ends.

He wrote a book on the seven habits of effective families, while his son Sean has published an adaptation called *The 7 Habits of Highly Effective Teens*. The publication of his book *The 8th Habit: From Effectiveness to Greatness* in 2004 also provoked a backlash.

In the afterword to the 2004 edition of *The 7 Habits of Highly Effective People*, Covey explains that, the way he sees it, the 8th habit is not an extra habit that was forgotten in the original work in 1989. On the contrary, it is a third dimension which aims to adapt the seven habits to the evolution of technology and the "Knowledge Worker Age". It therefore invites everyone to "find their voice" and encourage others to do the same.

SUMMARY

Stephen Covey's seven habits met with such resounding success because of their universal scope. Whether you want to improve your self-confidence, your relationship with your partner or your career, Covey's method offers a huge variety of very useful tools to make progress.

It can help you to become an independent, or perhaps even interdependent, person. As Covey himself sums it up, dependence means 'you', independence means 'I' and interdependence means 'we'. We therefore remain dependent as long as we need others to get what we want.

By implementing the first three habits, we become independent and can get what we want with our own efforts. Once we have acquired the second three habits, we reach the stage of interdependence, which means that we combine our efforts with other people's to achieve greater goals.

Summary of the different situations of dependence and in(ter)dependence

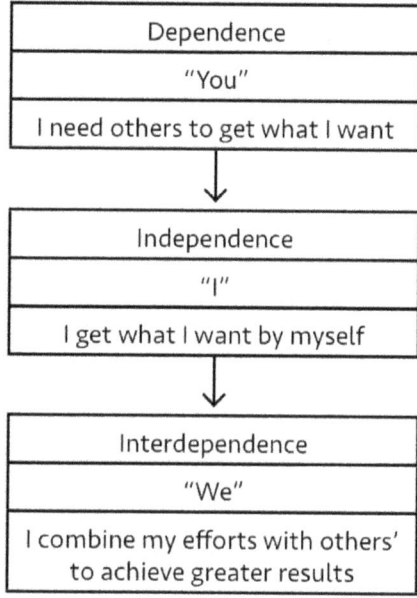

Dependence
"You"
I need others to get what I want

↓

Independence
"I"
I get what I want by myself

↓

Interdependence
"We"
I combine my efforts with others' to achieve greater results

© 50MINUTES.com

In Covey's opinion, modern society unfortunately puts greater emphasis on independence rather than interdependence. True personal effectiveness cannot just be limited to yourself: success requires a collective, collaborative dynamic, not just an individual one.

This dynamic is only possible if you adopt the seven habits and put them into practice in your everyday life:

- By being proactive and acting according to your moral values, which means choosing how to perceive and react

to external circumstances, whether good or bad.

- By being a leader, which means developing a personal mission statement which reflects your aspirations and values, thereby giving coherence and meaning to your actions.
- By learning to manage yourself with clear objectives. You therefore stop wasM time on unimportant tasks which will not help you to achieve your objectives.
- By adopting a win-win attitude and always looking for balance between your needs and the needs of others.
- By listening to others with a real sense of empathy and a desire to understand them. Listening should be done without judgement, without preparing your own answer and without forcing your own view down the other person's throat.
- By cooperating with others in a creative, open-minded way, while searching for synergy. This means that you have to value differences rather than fearing them.
- Finally, by constantly trying to improve yourself and becoming more interdependent in all aspects of your daily life.

Finally, you have to create an upward spiral which Covey sums up in three words: "learn, commit and do" (p. 200). "Learn" means opening your mind up to new things, "commit" means that you are the only one to decide on the changes to make in your life, and "do" means that you can only get results by anchoring change in your daily activities.

> "To learn and not to do is really not to learn. To know and not to do is really not to know." (Covey)

We want to hear from you!
Leave a comment on your online library
and share your favourite books on social media!

FURTHER READING

BIBLIOGRAPHY

- Blanchard, K. and Johnson, S. (1982) *The One Minute Manager*. New York: William Morrow and Company.
- Covey, S. (2004) *The 7 Habits of Highly Effective People*. New York: Free Press.
- Drucker, P. (2006) *The Effective Executive*. Oxford: Harper Business.
- El Sadat, A. (1978) *In Search of Identity*. Oxford: HarperCollins Publishers.
- Frankl, V. (2004) *Man's Search for Meaning*. Reading: Rider.
- Fisher, R. and Ury, W. (2012) *Getting to Yes*. London: Random House Business.
- FranklinCovey. [Online]. [Accessed 25 July 2017]. Available from: <https://www.franklincovey.com/>
- Franklin, B. (2015) *The Autobiography of Benjamin Franklin*. CreateSpace Independent Publishing Platform.
- Kuhn, T. (1996) *The Structure of Scientific Revolutions*. Chicago: University of Chicago Press.
- Lewin, K. (1943) Defining the Field at a Given Time. *Psychological Review*, 50(3), pp. 292-310.
- Project Happiness. [Online]. [Accessed 25 July 2017]. Available from: <https://projecthappiness.com/>
- Smith, H. (2008) *10 Natural Laws of Successful Time and Life Management*. New York: Business Plus.
- Stephen Covey's website. [Online]. [Accessed 25 July 2017]. Available from: <https://www.stephencovey.com/>

- Collins English Dictionary. (No date) *Synergy.*. [Online]. [Accessed 25 July 2017]. Available from: <https://www.collinsdictionary.com/dictionary/english/synergy>
- Wooldridge, A. (2002) Stephen Covey, RIP. *The Economist*. [Online]. [Accessed 25 July 2017]. Available from: <http://www.economist.com/node/21559329>

ADDITIONAL SOURCES

Other books by the same author

- Covey, S. (1999) *First Things First*. London: Simon & Schuster UK.
- Covey, S. (2012) *The Leader in Me: How Schools Around the World Are Inspiring Greatness, One Child at a Time*. New York: Simon & Schuster.
- Covey, S. (1999) *The 7 Habits Of Highly Effective Families*. London: Simon & Schuster UK.
- Covey, S. (2006) *The 8th Habit: From Effectiveness to Greatness*. London: Simon & Schuster UK.

Other sources

- Allen, D. (2015) *Getting Things Done: The Art of Stress-free Productivity*. London: Piatkus.
- Duckworth, A. (2017) *Grit: Why passion and resilience are the secrets to success*. London: Vermillion.
- Ferrazzi, K. (2014) *Never Eat Alone: And Other Secrets to Success, One Relationship at a Time*. London: Portfolio Penguin.

Videos

- AchievingConcepts. (2016) *7 Habits of Highly Effective People by Stephen Covey (Part 1)| Animated Book Review.* [Online]. [Accessed 25 July 2017]. Available from: <https://www.youtube.com/watch?v=qaJt6LTTcwY>
- FightMediocrity. (2015) *THE 7 HABITS OF HIGHLY EFFECTIVE PEOPLE BY STEPHEN COVEY - ANIMATED BOOK REVIEW.* [Online]. [Accessed 25 July 2017]. Available from: <https://www.youtube.com/watch?v=ktlTxC4QG8g>

www.50minutes.com

Ebook EAN: 9782808002684

Paperback EAN: 9782808002691

Legal Deposit: D/2017/12603/655

Cover: © Primento

Digital conception by Primento, the digital partner of publishers.

SUCCESS IS JUST A HABIT!

Find out all you need to know about *The 7 Habits of Highly Effective People* by Stephen R. Covey in under 50 minutes!

This book review and analysis is perfect for:

- Employees looking to get noticed in the workplace

- Negotiators who want to hone their trade

- Anyone who wants to enjoy better relationships with their colleagues and family

www.50minutes.com

Milton Keynes UK
Ingram Content Group UK Ltd.
UKHW021553280724
1054UKWH00020B/270